Module 1 • Set 2 • Unusual Libraries

CONTENTS

This book belongs to *Eliana*

GREAT MINDS

Great Minds® is the creator of *Eureka Math*®, *Wit & Wisdom*®, *Alexandria Plan*™, and *PhD Science*®.

Geodes® are published by Great Minds PBC in association with Wilson Language Training, publisher of *Fundations*®.

Credits

- *The Story Ship*: We want to extend our thanks to Thomas Brevik and the crew of the *Epos* for donating their photos to this book. You can learn even more about the Epos on its website: www.bokbaten.no/information-in-english/. More page: photo by Jan Miko/Shutterstock.com

- *A Library of Our Own*: More page: photo by EvgeniiAnd/Shutterstock.com

- *The Library of Fez*: front cover, iStock.com/hadynyah; back cover, More page, interior title page, p. 13 (right and bottom left), tile headers and footers, photos by Rebecca Trahan reprinted with permission; p. 2, Inu/Shutterstock.com; p. 3, Diego Grandi/Shutterstock.com; p. 4, Paul Street/Alamy Stock Photo; p. 5, age fotostock/Alamy Stock Photo; pp. 10–12, 14, photos by Aziza Chaouni reprinted with permission; p. 13 (top left), "Al-Karaouine Library, Fez, Morocco" by Martin Kalfatovic, courtesy Flickr, is licensed under the Creative Commons Attribution NonCommercial-ShareAlike 2.0 Generic (CC BY-NC-SA 2.0) license. Reprinted with permission.

greatminds.org

ISBN 978-1-64497-417-9

Printed in Mexico

1 2 3 4 5 6 7 8 9 10 QMX 27 26 25 24 23

LIBRARY CAT

by Marya Myers • illustrated by Neil Brigham

I am a cat,

a library cat.

It is a job for me

to check the books I see.

 2

No time to nap
or sit in a lap.

A bug or rat
is no pal to this cat.

No bug or rat
can whiz by this cat!

If I see a bug nip

at a scroll's tip,

I arch up my back,

tuck my chin, and . . . **WHACK!**

No bug or rat

can whiz by this cat!

No time to chat—

got to get rid of that rat.

When they whip by in a dash,
I tuck my chin and . . . **BASH!**

I am Anat,
the library cat.

12

No bug or rat

can whiz by this cat!

More

Alexandria is an Egyptian city on the edge of the Mediterranean Sea. Alexandria was famous for its library, which collected books from all over the world.

In ancient times, most books in the library were written on scrolls. A short book might be written on just one scroll. A long book might be written on many. Bugs and rats nibbled on the scrolls. Cats, just as they do today, chased pests away.

A fire destroyed the Library of Alexandria and all the books inside. The cause of the fire remains a mystery. Although the original library is no more, modern libraries still hold important books. Library cats continue to roam freely in some libraries even to this day.

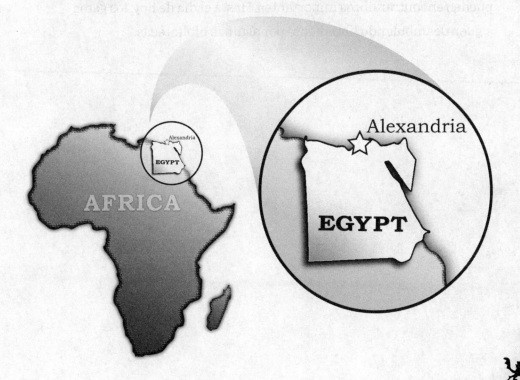

Más

Alejandría es una ciudad de Egipto cuyas costas tocan el mar Mediterráneo. Alejandría fue muy famosa por una biblioteca que tenía una colección de libros de todas partes del mundo.

Antiguamente, la mayoría de los libros se escribían en pergaminos. Es probable que un libro corto se escribiera en un solo pergamino. Un libro largo podría escribirse en varios pergaminos. Los insectos y las ratas mordisqueaban estos pergaminos. Los gatos ahuyentaban las plagas, tal como sucede hoy en día.

Un incendio destruyó la biblioteca de Alejandría junto con todos sus libros. La causa del incendio sigue siendo un misterio. A pesar de que la biblioteca original ya no existe, en las bibliotecas modernas aún se pueden encontrar libros importantes. Hasta el día de hoy, los gatos siguen deambulando libremente por algunas bibliotecas.

◢THE◣
STORY SHIP

story by Emily Climer

drawings by Julia Stojsic • photographs by Thomas Brevik

This is a ship.

But it is not *any* ship.

This

    is a ship

        with a story.

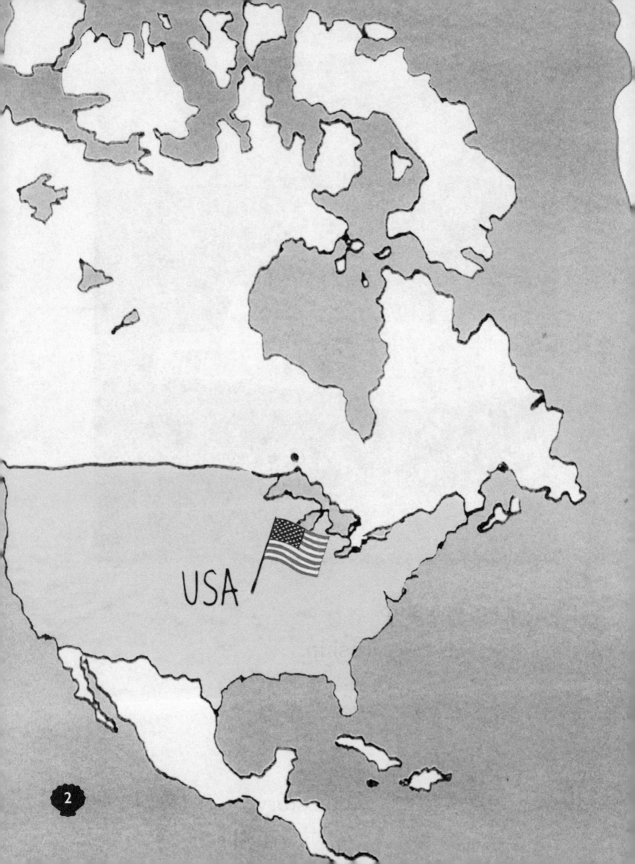

USA

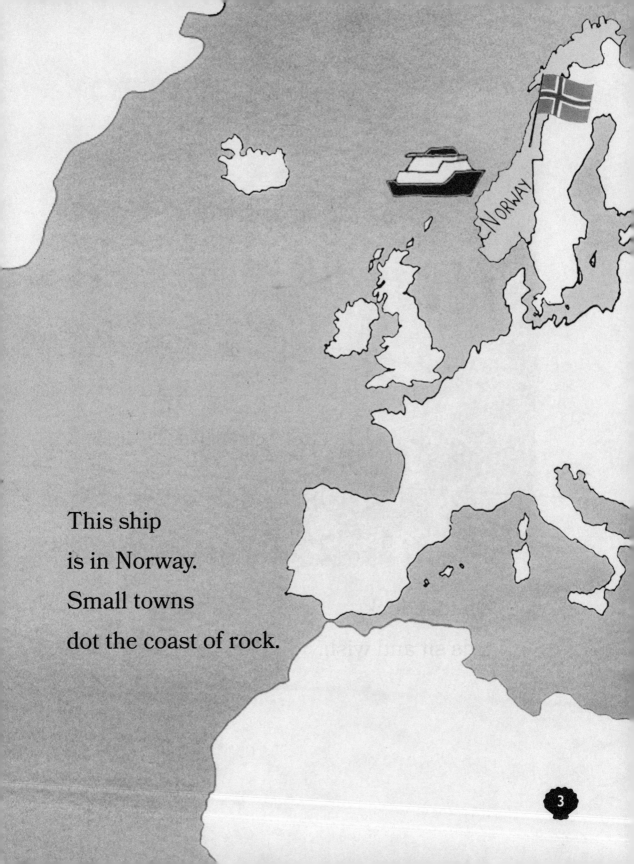

This ship
is in Norway.
Small towns
dot the coast of rock.

On this dock,

kids sit and wish.

The ship pulls up

to the dock.

They run on to see . . .

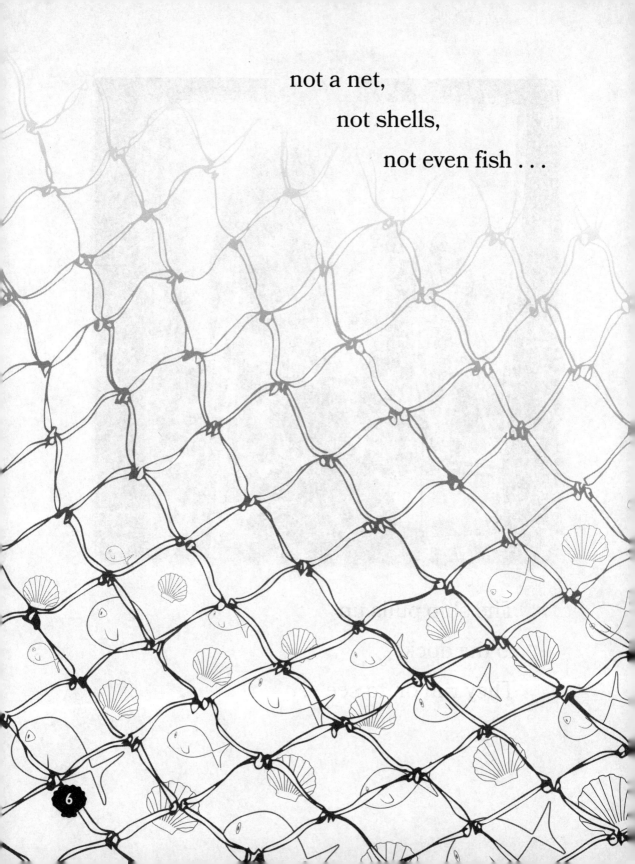

not a net,

not shells,

not even fish . . .

6

but bin
after bin
of books!

This
is the ship
with a story.
This is the Story Ship!

They call it the *Epos*.

On this ship,

you are rich with books.

You sit.

You read.

You chat with a pal.

This kid

has a book bud

on the Story Ship.

They kick back

and have a lot of fun.

Tip, dip—TIP, DIP!

Now and then,

big waves rock the ship.

Books fall with a thud.

But this is not a shock.

They pick them up,

one by one,

until the job is done.

Then, it is time

for the ship to move on.

This ship has more stories to tell.

For this is the Story Ship—

a library on the waves.

More

The real ship featured in this book is called the *Epos*. The ship is 85 feet long and carries 6,000 books. From September through April, it delivers books to readers in 150 remote communities along the western coast of Norway.

Thomas Brevik, a librarian on the boat since 1990, shared some of the photographs in this book. They show part of a 45-day book tour and the beauty of the Norwegian fjords. Fjords are narrow slivers of ocean between steep rocky cliffs. They were carved millions of years ago by rivers of ice.

Getting to libraries can be hard for people who live near the fjords. Thankfully, the *Epos* is able to navigate the waters to bring books, puppet shows, and author visits to these communities.

Más

El verdadero barco del que habla este libro se llama *Epos*. El barco mide 85 pies de largo y alberga 6,000 libros. Desde septiembre hasta abril, entrega libros a lectores de 150 comunidades remotas a lo largo de la costa occidental de Noruega.

Thomas Brevik, quien ha sido bibliotecario en este barco desde 1990, compartió algunas de las fotografías de este libro. En ellas se observa parte del recorrido de 45 días, así como la belleza de los fiordos de Noruega. Los fiordos son entradas del mar muy estrechas, entre acantilados rocosos y escarpados. Se formaron hace millones de años por la acción de los ríos de hielo.

El acceso a las bibliotecas puede ser difícil para las personas que viven cerca de los fiordos. Afortunadamente, *Epos* puede navegar las aguas para ofrecer libros, espectáculos de títeres y visitas de autores a estas comunidades.

A Library of Our Own

written by
Ashley Davis Hymel

illustrated by
Mathieu Persan

I have a wish.
I wish to run a library
with my pals.

Books thick and thin,
we love them all!

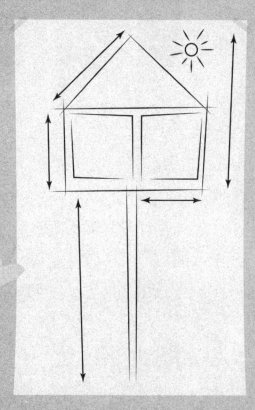

OUR LIBRARY

Step by step,

we can set up a library

of our own.

1. Set a plan.

We pick a spot.

It is fun to chat and draw!

2. Check with Mom or Dad.

I run the plan
by Mom and Dad.
They nod.

YES!

5

3. Get what we need.

We dash
to the shed
in the back.

We pick a big box
and some tin.
It is a fit!

4. Fix it up.

We cut a door
in the box.

Then,
we set the tin
on top.
Whack, whack!
Tap, tap!

5. Add color.

We paint the box red.

With a rag,

we rub on wax.

This is so the books

do not get wet.

6. Get books.

We pick books to share.

We have books on

art,

       a dog,

            a math whiz,

and how to be a vet!

We tuck them in the box.

7. Set up shop.

We tack a sign
to the box.
We have set up shop!

We did it!

OUR LIBRARY

Open!

★ Daily News ★

NEW LIBRARY
OPENS!

13

In time,
the library grows.
Books zip in,
and books
rush out.

Thick or thin,
we love them all!

OUR LIBRARY

14

More

More than 16,000 U.S. public libraries provide free access to books. One of the oldest ones is in Darby, Pennsylvania. It opened in 1743 and remains open today.

A Library of Our Own is inspired by another type of library. Little Free Libraries® help neighbors share books. To start this type of library, people can order finished libraries or kits. They can also build their own library boxes. In 2016, there were more than 50,000 Little Free Libraries® in the world.

Little Free Library is a registered trademark of Little Free Library LTD, a nonprofit organization.

Más

Más de 16,000 bibliotecas públicas en Estados Unidos brindan acceso gratuito a libros. Una de las más antiguas se encuentra en Darby, Pensilvania. Se inauguró en 1743 y sigue abierta hasta el día de hoy.

El libro *A Library of Our Own* (*Una biblioteca propia*) se inspira en otro tipo de biblioteca. Las *Little Free Libraries*® son pequeñas bibliotecas que se ubican en los hogares para ayudar a los vecinos a compartir libros. Para tener este tipo de biblioteca en la casa, se puede comprar el juego de piezas para armarla o pedir la cajuela que ya viene construida. También se pueden construir las bibliotecas con cajas. En 2016 había más de 50,000 *Little Free Libraries*® en todo el mundo.

Read Along

Read this text aloud as the young reader follows along.
This knowledge-building text includes a number of words
that the young reader may not yet know how to read.

The Library of Fez

by Emily Climer & Michelle Palmieri • illustrated by Jordi Solano

•Fez

Morocco

Pack a bag,
come with me,
into the city of Fez.

Check and look
at the tile and rock.
Sit with the art of Fez.

3

Dash into

the library,

on the path in Fez.

Books of old,

rich as gold,

sit in the library of Fez.

6

Back in time,

a big, thick door

hid the books of Fez.

The door was shut

with a 4-key lock

to guard the books of Fez.

It took 4 men,

each with one key,

to open the lock of Fez.

A tick and a click.

When the keys fit . . .

. . . books!

For the people of Fez.

The door is still open
to sit and read.
Pick a book from Fez!

Not just 4 men,

but all who read,

protect the books of Fez.

The books are here

for you and me.

They are the riches of Fez.

The library is strong.

The books live on.

Live on for the people of Fez.

More

More than 1,000 years ago, a woman named Fatima Al-Fihri donated money to build a university in Fez, Morocco. She wanted it to be a center of learning. The university later added a library. For centuries, scholars gathered within its walls. It is one of the oldest libraries in the world.

Over time, the building decayed. In 2012, the architect Aziza Chaouni began to restore the library. She modernized the library to keep the books dry and added a lab to repair books. Much of the library changed, but one part stayed the same. The special metal door with four locks is still a part of the library. Today, visitors from around the world enjoy the beauty and bounty of the library of Fez.

Más

Hace más de 1,000 años, una mujer llamada Fatima Al-Fihri donó fondos para construir una universidad en Fez, Marruecos. Quería que fuera un centro de enseñanza. Posteriormente, se incorporó una biblioteca a la universidad. Durante siglos, los académicos se reunían en este edificio. Es una de las bibliotecas más antiguas del mundo.

Con el paso del tiempo, el edifició se deterioró. En 2012, la arquitecta Aziza Chaouni comenzó a restaurar la biblioteca. La modernizó para que los libros se mantuvieran secos y también incorporó un laboratorio para reparar libros. La mayor parte de la biblioteca sufrió modificaciones, pero una parte permaneció tal como estaba. La biblioteca sigue teniendo una puerta especial de metal con cuatro cerrojos. Actualmente, recibe visitantes de todas partes del mundo que disfrutan la belleza y abundancia de la biblioteca de Fez.